The Shaman's Nephew

A Life in the Far North

Simon Tookoome with Sheldon Oberman

Stoddart Kids

TORONTO • NEW YORK

Acknowledgements

Simon Tookoome and I wish to thank those who helped with the translation: Harry Niakrok, Steven Kigusiutnak, and Margret Gibbons of Arviat; Eva Klassen of Iqaliut; Betty Amaruq Hughson in Winnipeg; Daniel Piryuaq and Elizabeth Keyouayou of Baker Lake; Grace and Johnny Tookoome; and especially Nancy Tookoome who helped from the very start to the very end of this book. Canada Council and the Manitoba Arts Council have also given generous support.

Photos: The Inuit Art Section of the Department of Indian Affairs and Northern Development and the Arctic Cooperatives provided slides. Most came to them from the Sanavik Cooperative. There are no records of who took the photos but Simon Tookoome, the artist, holds the copyright.

Published in Canada in 1999 by
Stoddart Kids,
a division of Stoddart Publishing Co. Limited
895 Don Mills Road, 400–2 Park Centre
Toronto, ON M3C 1W3
Tel (416) 445-3333 Fax (416) 445-5967
E-mail cservice@genpub.com

Distributed in Canada by
General Distribution Services
325 Humber College Blvd.,
Toronto, ON M9W 7C3
Tel (416) 213-1919 Fax (416) 213-1917
E-mail cservice@genpub.com

Published in the United States in 2000 by
Stoddart Kids,
a division of Stoddart Publishing Co. Limited
180 Varick Street, 9th Floor
New York, New York 10014
Toll free 1-800-805-1083
E-mail gdsinc@genpub.com

Distributed in the United States by
General Distribution Services, PMB 128
4500 Witmer Industrial Estates
Niagara Falls, New York 14305-1386
Toll free 1-800-805-1083
E-mail gdsinc@genpub.com

04 03 02 01 00 2 3 4 5 6

Canadian Cataloguing in Publication Data

Tookoomee, Simon
The shaman's nephew : a life in the far North

ISBN 0-7737-3200-4 (bound)   ISBN 0-7737-6189-6 (pbk.)

1. Tookoome, Simon. 2. Inuit – Nunavut – Baker Lake – Social life and customs – Juvenile literature.
3. Inuit – Nunavut – Baker Lake – Biography – Juvenile literature.
4. Inuit artists – Nunavut – Baker Lake – Biography – Juvenile literature. I. Oberman, Sheldon. II. Title.

E99.E7T665 1999   j971.9'4   C99-930978-1

The lifestyle, customs, and beliefs of the traditional Inuit, as related by artist Simon Tookoome, depict life in the North as it used to be.

We acknowledge for their financial support of our publishing program the Canada Council, the Ontario Arts Council, and the Government of Canada through the Book Publishing Industry Development Program (BPIDP).

Printed in Hong Kong, China

To Jesse Paul Shoshon Tookoome Dveris-Oberman
from his father, Sheldon Oberman,
and his name giver, Simon Tookoome.

Introduction

Simon Tookoome was one of the last of the Inuit to live the traditional nomadic life in the Far North. (Inuit, which means *the people*, is what they call themselves rather than Eskimo, which is a foreign name.) Though the Inuit had only Stone Age tools they were brilliantly adapted to the harsh conditions of the Arctic. They remained nomads travelling with the seasons until the 1960s when they were forced to settle in government-built towns.

Tookoome (he prefers to be called by his traditional Inuit name) resisted government efforts to make him leave the land. He continued to follow the caribou and the seals, feeding and clothing his family from the land. However, he, too, was eventually compelled to join the rest of his people, and he now lives in the settlement of Baker Lake near the Arctic Circle west of Hudson Bay.

Nevertheless, he has kept his sled dogs and continues to hunt to feed his family. He has also kept his language and speaks only Inuktitut. His people know him as a skillful hunter, a respected elder and justice of the peace, a drum dancer, and a master of the forty-foot whip. The world knows him as an artist whose works are shown internationally. The picture that falls on page 55 also graces a Canadian stamp.

Tookoome is a leading artist from a generation of great Inuit artists. Remarkably, the Inuit had never before created art. They did not even have a word for it. Their art developed during their time of great change as they entered the modern world. For some, art was simply a product to sell but for others like Tookoome, it was also a way to express an ancient way of living and perceiving. And so Tookoome has created a body of art that is strange and wonderful. His story is equally strange and wonderful.

It may seem surprising that Tookoome chose me to tell his story. I am not Inuit. I am not even from the North. I am a Jewish writer and storyteller from the North End of Winnipeg. In 1989, I was invited to tour as an author through a part of the Northwest Territories which is now called Nunavut. The tour was in the spring. At least, it was spring-time in Winnipeg. It was still winter up North, and though I didn't like the thought of enduring any more winter, I was intrigued. Few people ever get to see the Far North. It was a once-in-a-lifetime opportunity. I agreed to go but I asked to stay with a traditional Inuit family. I wanted to learn about those remarkable people who had lived since ancient times in that vast and dangerous land.

I packed my warmest clothes. I read a stack of books. I even found someone who had been up North and would answer my questions. And when I arrived I was completely unprepared.

I started my journey from Winnipeg in a four-propeller Lockheed Electra. It could have held eighty passengers but most of the seats had been removed and the space was used for cargo. It was the kind of plane where you kept your coat on and plugged your ears. We flew north for more than a thousand miles and entered the Keewatin Region, far beyond the tree line, a quarter million square miles of frozen desert uninhabited except for six thousand Inuit and a scattering of Kabloonaq (white people), few of whom stay for long.

As I disembarked in Rankin Inlet, I thought the plane's propellers were still roaring until I realized that I was hearing the howl of the Arctic wind; a wind that blew day and night with nothing to stop it for thousands of miles except for this tiny settlement. It had pushed the snow into huge drifts higher than the houses. It had buried the Mountie station so I could see only the station's tattered Canadian flag flapping on a pole with half the maple leaf worn away.

I'd been told about the Arctic blizzards that could blast snow through the finest cracks in any house, filtering into hallways and cupboards. I'd been told about the danger even within town: a person had frozen to death walking home from the store, and others on a snowmobile had been so blinded by the blowing snow that they missed their house at the edge of town and could not find their way back. This wasn't even a blizzard, yet I was soon totally unnerved and frozen to the bone. I quickly transferred into a four-seater Cessna 172 and we headed even farther north.

Arriving at Baker Lake, I didn't notice Tookoome standing by the runway. He was such a quiet, unassuming man and he stood so still and calm despite the cold. He, on the other hand, had no difficulty recognizing me. I was ridiculously out of place wearing a city coat and loaded down with my Apple 2E computer, an airport suitcase on wheels, and four boxes of books I'd brought for my book signings. Eventually he stepped forward with a great smile and silently motioned me into his sled. He loaded me in along with my boxes and cases and covered me with blankets, and off we went over the frozen drifts. I must have looked like strange cargo.

He looked strange to me as well. I had wanted to stay with a true Inuk or "true Inuit hunter." Tookoome was that and more. He spoke no English. His hands were rough and his face was deeply etched by the elements. The entrance to his home looked like a burrow in the snow surrounded by his yelping huskies. Once inside, I saw that it was a long, government-built mobile divided into rooms. It was clean, warm, and very sparse. I reminded myself that in a nomadic culture, people didn't accumulate needless objects. Possessions had to be transported from site to site so nonessentials were quickly left behind. There was very little furniture in Tookoome's home and the only "art" was a Hudson's Bay calendar. Yet amazingly, there was a big screen TV playing Home Box Office.

Tookoome sat me in front of the TV. He boiled some black tea and fried up a delicious bannock for bread. He then generously brought out the imported southern Canadian delicacy that he had bought for me as his guest so I would feel more at home. It was a ten-pound piece of unsliced baloney.

We ate together in front of the TV and we watched a movie called *Sheena*. In the movie, Sheena was presented as a blonde jungle woman who had been raised by animals and spent her time riding a zebra bareback through the luscious greenery. Tookoome, a real hunter and nomad, seemed to be thoroughly enjoying this phony Hollywood version. Yet after a while, I realized that Tookoome and I weren't even sharing that simple experience. I was watching Sheena. He was watching the zebra. Whenever an animal appeared Tookoome became intent, studying it as carefully as he would a caribou or a polar bear on the tundra.

The house was always busy with people. Tookoome and his wife had eleven grown children who came and went, and there were many visits from neighbours and friends. There was not a lot of English spoken but everyone was friendly and curious. They may have been impressed that I was an author on tour, but they were most certainly delighted by the baloney, which soon ran out.

I then turned to traditional Inuit food, raw caribou meat. A freshly killed caribou, quartered and stripped, was kept on a sheet of cardboard on the kitchen floor. Tookoome indicated with a smile and an open hand that I was welcome to eat all I wanted. I simply had to cut pieces off the leg with a crescent-shaped ulu knife. But it had to be eaten raw. That had been the secret of Inuit survival. Raw caribou meat contained most of the nutrients a body needed, nutrients that could not otherwise be found in a land without fruit except for some scarce berries, no milk products, grain and almost no vegetation. However, if the meat was cooked, it lost those essential vitamins. I tried it. The meat was tender with a strong but almost pleasant venison taste. I learned to eat it but I could never develop an appetite for it.

In that unforgiving climate without a common language or familiar food, things began to feel very foreign to me, more foreign than anywhere I'd visited in Europe or the Middle East or beyond. I was in Canada, my own country, yet I was experiencing culture shock.

Then Nancy, one of Tookoome's older daughters, arrived and she began to translate in her thoughtful, patient way. First Tookoome and I greeted each other properly and explained who we were and how we lived, the common courtesies. As the conversation lengthened he brought out his art, drawn on paper with coloured pencils (having no desk or easel, he drew on a board while lying on his bed). I was amazed at the images. They seemed to float and shift from shape to shape. His work had such compelling power, the primal beauty of a cave painting, the imagination of a modern Miro or Chagall. I was charmed but bewildered. His images were as foreign to me as his Inuktitut words.

"Let me tell you about my pictures," he said through Nancy. "The pictures have stories. This picture shows how it was when we hunted. There is the wolf I adopted. He became my friend and he helped me hunt. Most dogs don't live more than two or three years in this cold, but my wolf was strong. In this next picture a shaman is flying. He is moving across the land using his magic. He had told me that he would visit and show me his power. Here I am watching him fly over my tent and I am surprised. In the next picture, the people are singing in the great igloo that we call a *qaggiq*. Each person has his own special song. My mother was a Keeper of Songs for the people." Tookoome then sang his mother's wolf song.

I was delighted and moved. I responded with my own stories and stories of my people from Jewish history and folklore. I was no longer a stranger in a strange world. I was a storyteller   7 sharing tales with another of my kind.

Yet I was not the only one who was hearing Tookoome's stories for the first time. Some of them were new to his daughter Nancy. Tookoome explained. "In the past," he said, "our stories were told too often to count. Everyone knew all the stories. It is no longer that way."

I asked him what had changed. Was it because of the TV? Has it stopped the people from telling their stories? Are they too absorbed by the stories from Hollywood and New York? It went further than that for Tookoome. "It is the walls," he said. "In the igloo there were no walls. In these buildings we are separated. We do not see or hear each other. We have become different."

Stories are not being passed on. Nor is the sense of art. The next generation does not have the same skills. They were born in the settlements, taught in the public or residential schools. They grew up with machines and electric appliances. Most of their food is bought in a store. They and their parents live together in the same small place yet the new generation lives and perceives quite differently.

Before I left, Tookoome asked me if I would write a book about his life on the land. He said he could not find anyone among his people to do it. He was concerned that his stories would be lost. He wanted the young people of the future to know how the Inuit had lived. I hesitated. I was an ignorant outsider, not even what they call a "hardly know it." I didn't even know how to walk on that land. The Inuit children laughed when they saw me walk head down in a straight line as if I was on a city sidewalk. Inuit follow the subtle contours of the land with their heads up, searching the horizon. I told Tookoome that I was not the right person for the job. He was not worried. I could do what was needed, he said. I could listen and I could tell a story well. With help, a great deal of help, I could tell his story.

Over the next ten years, I interviewed him many times. I had him repeat his stories and explain his experiences in various ways until they gradually found a form and a life on the page. I deliberately used many different translators. Sometimes a new translation brought out new information, but, just as importantly, each translator told the stories differently. A social worker, a labourer, a teacher, a medical translator, relatives, and family members — each translated from a particular perspective. My task was to interview, research, select, and shape but it was also to merge the different translations into a common voice, Tookoome's voice. I have hunted hard for it. I hope I have found it.

We call this book *The Shaman's Nephew* because Tookoome's uncle was a shaman and he wanted Tookoome to follow him. However, the way of the shaman was coming to an end. Tookoome did not take up the shaman's magic to become a seer and healer, a spirit hunter who transforms himself to join with creatures of the land and the sea.

Yet Tookoome has found another way to become a transformer, a seer, and a healer. He has found the way of the artist. He hunts spirits and joins with creatures through his imagination and skill. He draws them out and they appear on paper, strange and wonderful. He becomes a seer as he shows us an extraordinary world with his extraordinary eyes. He becomes a healer as he reminds his people what they have been and what the land still offers. This book containing his stories and art is an heirloom to his people and a great gift to all of us.

Sheldon Oberman 1999

◆ SUMMER CAMP PEOPLE

Being Born

I remember being born. I was born on the land while we were travelling by foot along the shore of the Arctic Ocean. It was summer. I do not know what year it was. Perhaps 1934. Inuit did not use large numbers or calendars to know the time. So my mother could not tell me the year.

But I remember coming out of my mother's body. I remember seeing how the land looked. The day was very beautiful and hot. I could see people all around me, and there were many dogs with loads on their backs. I thought it would always be that time — with the same weather and the same people always with me.

My parents and my two uncles were my family. I was the only child in their igloo. At my birth they rubbed the skin of the seagull over my eyes so that when I became a hunter, I would have good eyesight.

There was also an old man living with us, one of my mother's elder relatives. He became my *Inuk Hanayuq* — the person who makes the name. He holds the newborn baby and says how its character will grow. This is a blessing with great power. My *Inuk Hanayuq* said that my words would be strong and the people would listen to them. His spirit still protects me and guides me. I often feel him giving strength to my words. No one told me what he had predicted for me, not until it began to come true.

The Edge of the World

We call ourselves Inuit, which means "the people." Eskimo is the name we were called by others. We did not have schools. We learned everything from the land.

We learned about time from the sky, not from clocks. During the day, the sun told us the time as it crossed the sky. At night we looked at the whole sky. We watched for when the moon came out and went away again. And when the different stars appeared and disappeared. The sky was our clock.

We never used a compass. We looked at the way the wind shaped the snow. The wind generally blows in one steady direction, from north to south. So there were hardened snowdrifts that showed which way was north and south. At night the stars told us the directions.

Animals and stones kept us warm. Our stove was a carved stone filled with caribou fat. The fat would burn with a low flame, almost like a candle, but it was enough to keep us warm. We did not always use matches to light a fire. We made fire by striking pyrite stones. The stones would spark. Other Inuit rubbed wood with a leather bow string to kindle a fire.

Everything we wore was made from animals. Almost everything we ate was from the animals, as well. Generally we ate the meat raw. We still do. Raw meat has much greater nourishment. It is not necessary to cook it. Animals in the north do not have germs because of the extreme cold.

When I was very young, the people still relied on bows and spears. They had a few guns but most of them were not much good for hunting. Some were old muskets that had to be loaded through the barrel. They were very loud and smoky.

The Seasons

♦ A TIME OF PLENTY

In the winter the people lived inland in small family groups. They hunted the caribou and the fox. Whoever did not have enough caches of meat would live by the ocean. In January and February they hunted for seals.

By March and April the people began joining together as all the families made their way to the spring camp along the ocean. By May and June a great many people were camping together. We would fish and we would hunt the birds.

By August the people separated again into small groups. Most went back inland to hunt the caribou for clothing. There would not yet be snow so the dogs had to carry the loads on their backs. Once the snow was good again, the dogs were joined together to pull the sled. The people knew the routes of the caribou and would travel to meet them. Everyone would run beside the dog sled all day long, but the little children would be wrapped up on the sled. I was small so they kept me in the sled. I thought that we were travelling to the edge of the world. I wondered what we would do when we got there.

Names

My parents were named after their parents. My mother was named Kiligvak — it is an animal with a horn like a rhinoceros that is believed to live under the ground. My father was called Hiuttinuaq, which means little ears. My stepfather was called Tutanuak, which means the part of the head behind the temple.

My grandfather (my mother's father) died before I was born but he wanted me to have his name: Tookoome. No one knows what that name means anymore.

Our name decides our nature. If a child is named after an elder, then it is believed that the nature of that elder enters and shapes the child's character. Even if the child is named after someone who is dead, the spirit of the name giver enters the child and everyone treats the child as they had treated the name giver.

My granddaughter is named Kajurjuk after my younger sister who is dead. Her spirit moves through her. She speaks and acts like my sister. To me, my granddaughter is my sister. I do things for her as if my sister was asking. I am always respectful. If someone yells at her, I will defend her because she is both my granddaughter and my sister.

Sometimes the name can cause the very opposite nature. My grandfather decided that since he was too shy he wanted me to be the opposite of him. He told

♦ THE CHILDREN BECOME THE RACES

my parents to teach me not to be shy like him but to put myself forward. He gave me his name so it would shape my nature in that way.

Often names come from dreams. The Inuit believe that the spirit of a dead elder may send a dream to tell parents what to name a child. Some people will not listen or will not understand. They will decide on a different name. That can cause problems. A child may become sick and no one will be able to find a cure. The parents must learn what the child's proper name should be. Changing the name may bring the child out of the illness.

Before the Kabloonaq (white people), no one had a family name. My name was just Tookoome. The Church came when I was a young man and gave all the people Christian names. They called me Simon. Now my name is Simon Tookoome.

15

♦ OCEAN SIDE

Living on the Ocean Side

My mother was from the Ukusiksalingmiut tribe (soapstone people). My father was from the Ki'liniqmuit tribe (people of the sea edge). My family would spend the spring and summer along the shore of the Arctic Ocean around Chantrey Inlet.

I was used to sea animals — especially the many kinds of seals. I remember eating the raw intestine and liver of the bearded seal. They were good. The seal blubber was used for both food and heating fuel. We didn't have kayaks. We hunted the seals in the spring ice at their breathing holes.

We went to the trading post with the skins from the fox, wolf, and caribou. Also caribou sinew. We traded them to the Kabloonaq for tea, tobacco, bullets, biscuits, a bit of sugar, lard, and flour.

During the winter we could travel across the frozen water to the trading post. We got tea and other supplies until the spring melt came in July. Then we would have to wait until December when the ocean became frozen again. We would go back to drinking caribou soup or tea from berries. We melted snow for tea by building small fires with the moss and small branches that grew along the ground.

Some folks got the smoking habit from the Kabloonaq. They would have the hardest time waiting. They would grind old tobacco out of their pipes and search for bits in their pockets.

Sometimes the trading post ran out of supplies. Then it was very hard because everyone had grown to need the white people's supplies.

How We Were Raised

Inuit don't like to eat alone. We call people to our homes and we all eat together. It feels better to share food. When a person had a successful hunt he would call everyone to share the food. This also happened when a child first caught something. The family would cut it into small pieces and call everyone to share it. This made the child very proud. When I caught my first snow goose, everyone was very happy. They celebrated by tearing it into pieces to share with everyone. The pieces were so small there was almost nothing of the goose. But everyone got something.

Once my friends and I were playing far from camp. We caught and killed some baby geese. We brought them back to show everyone. We were proud that we had killed something like hunters. My parents did not get angry but they explained that when we got big we could catch birds to eat but we must not hurt the little ones. We understood that we must never kill something unless we needed to.

My parents were never angry with me. Anger and impatience were the worst things for Inuit. It was dangerous to behave that way on the land. If you lost your reason you could have an accident or get lost. It was also dangerous in the igloo. The people had to live closely together for long periods of time. They needed to get along with each other.

Inuit parents believed that if they acted with anger, the child would turn away and act with anger. If they spoke with respect, the child would learn respect.

♦ HAPPY PEOPLE

We did not ask questions. To ask a question was considered rude. We waited to find things out. We learned by being quiet and watching. This is still true even as adults.

Sometimes someone might tell a person how to do something but no one gave an order unless it was very serious. When decisions had to be made, we would talk together until we all agreed. We did not boss each other around — we did not have bosses. We were all families living together.

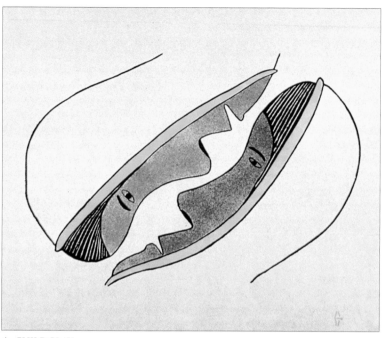

♦ CHILD PLAY

Adventures With My Friend

My best friend was Siquaq. We were never separate except to sleep. We would always help each other and teach each other.

My friend and I made a game of grabbing frozen pieces of fish out of each other's mouths. We ate roe and trout. I loved a fresh fish. I'd pull it out of the water and hit it on the head. It froze very quickly in the cold air. Then I'd cut it up and eat it raw.

My favourite thing to do was to slide down the snow hills. I had a pair of sealskin pants that were very slippery on the snow. We would also make a sled out of ice to slide on. In the summer we would run through the ponds and get wet.

20

We played many games like high kicking or one-hand reach, where you would lift your body on one hand and reach up with the other hand. We had pulling contests — pulling each other by the hand or by the head.

In the igloo we would attach a rope of bearded sealskin through the walls, holding it tightly in place with caribou legs. Then we would balance on the rope and perform tricks. Balancing and acrobatics on a sealskin rope are called *uyautaut*.

We would also have spearing contests. We would try to spear a hole in a bone that was hanging from an igloo ceiling. There was also a game called *ajagak* — trying to poke the hole of a spindle with the point of a bone.

We also made a little harpoon, called a *kakivak*, that had a sharp blade of bone. It would stick into fish. We played with a sling called an *illut*. Once I got a cut in my head from throwing a stone with my sling. I hit a caribou antler. It bounced back and hit me in the head. My friend carried me home.

Siquaq and I visited each other even when we were camped far away on different sides of the lake. Sometimes I would sneak out of our igloo early in the morning. I ran the distance in about half an hour. I knew the way well and there were no dangers. My parents did not get upset. They knew how important my friend was to me.

Our families would move to different hunting grounds during the winters. I would not see Siquaq again for many months. It hurt to say goodbye. Together we two boys learned about friendship.

The Whip

When I was eight years old my father and my uncle made me a whip from the skin of a bearded seal. We used the whip to direct the dogs as they pulled the sled. We didn't hit them. We just cracked the whip at the side and the dogs would turn. If the dogs started to fight, I would use the whip handle to separate them.

When I was twelve I would borrow my father's long whip and slip out while everyone was asleep. I did not want my mother to see me use the long whip. I practised on bits of antlers. Then I learned to use it to hunt ptarmigans. I would sneak up and whip off their heads. I often came back with five or six birds.

As I grew, the whips they made for me grew as well until I had a whip forty feet long. By that time I had a rifle. But when I ran out of bullets I used the whip to hunt caribou. I chased caribou in the sled and when they got too tired to run, I walked alongside them until I was close enough. I would strike a caribou on the legs with the whip or else I would catch the antlers. I then grabbed the caribou and killed it with a knife. Often I could strike at the ear and that would be enough. The caribou would fall down stunned and I would finish it off.

♦ I AM ALWAYS THINKING OF ANIMALS

Watching Animals

I like to watch animals, not only to hunt them. I want to understand them. When I am with other Inuit, we always talk about what the animals are doing. I am always thinking of animals.

When I was a child I was afraid of wolves and polar bears. I learned not to be afraid. Wolves will run away. They are only dangerous if they are in a pack. Even then they will not bother people unless they are attacked.

Polar bears can be dangerous. They will enter an igloo to attack a person. The dogs will generally keep them away.

Wolverines can be dangerous as well, even though they are smaller than dogs. A single wolverine can kill a muskox. It jumps on the ox's back and holds on by the teeth. It keeps biting until the ox dies. Wolverines are dangerous but they are also very rare.

23

My Adopted Animals

My parents would bring me young animals so that I would understand them better when I had to hunt them. Once my parents even brought home a very young polar bear. They told me not to hurt these animals, just to play with them.

When I got older I adopted caribou, ducks, wolves, all kinds of animals. It was a good way to learn about animals. Later the government made it against the law to adopt any wild animals. But I always think of them.

My adopted caribou would follow me like a dog. It would not leave even when I set it free. The ducks would fly south in the fall because if they did not, their legs would freeze from the cold.

I have adopted five wolves at different times. They are more loving than dogs. I had one wolf that I loved very much. I found it as a pup. I named it Amaruq, which means wolf. Amaruq was very protective of me. He would guard me from other dogs or wolves or people that he did not know. I could not even play at wrestling with a person or with another dog because Amaruq would become very upset. I only had to say something and Amaruq would fight to protect me. He would also lie down and be still if I told him.

He always obeyed me. When I hunted a caribou, I would get close and crouch down. Amaruq would crouch beside me. He could chase down a wounded caribou and grab its throat. He knew exactly where to attack. He did not need to be trained.

Amaruq would carry meat on his back. Wolves are smarter and bigger than dogs.

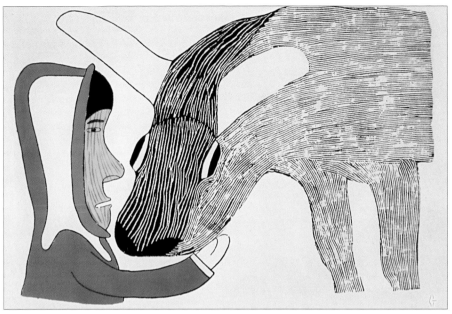

♦ FRIENDSHIP

They are strong but it is hard to get them to pull a sled. Except Amaruq. I put him on the left side of the lead dog so he could learn to be a lead dog. The dogs got used to him and accepted him.

Amaruq had very fine fur. Everyone wanted it. People would say, "Can I have his fur when he is dead?" One day I left Amaruq tied up and went off to hunt. He broke away and tried to find me but he came too close to another camp. He wore a collar, and they could see he was tame, but someone shot him for his fur. When I found out what happened I cried. Then I became angry. I wanted to shoot that person's dog. My mother talked to me. She said, "Anger is useless." I listened to her and I let my anger go. I made the man pay me for the wolf but I did not take revenge. I still feel sad when I think of losing Amaruq.

♦ SKINNING AFTER A HUNT

Hunting

Sometimes when hunting we would walk from six in the morning until dark with a heavy pack. We'd only stop twice. We might keep going like this for as long as five days at a time.

When the Inuit walk over the snow, the snow does not get on them. Inuit know how to travel with the snow. We do not walk across the snow in a straight line, but rather we walk the way that the land moves. And as we walk we look up at the horizon, not down at the path. We are always looking for animals.

We'd howl in order to trick the wolves. That was how we got close enough to catch them. We hunted them for their fur.

With seals we lay on the ice and scraped with our hands like a seal does. The seals thought we were creatures like them and let us get closer. Often we hunted seals at a breathing hole, called an *aglu*. Sometimes we had to wait a whole day for a seal to come. The ice was very thick and the hole got a salty snow covering from the sea water, so you could not see the seal coming up to breathe. We used a down feather or rabbit fluff suspended over the *aglu* to spot the seal's breath. Or we used a long thin bone as a bob to see how high the seal was rising. The seal pushed up the bob as it rose to the surface. We thrust the spear into the hole to hit the seal. Then we held onto the spear with a rope looped around our hands as the seal fought to get away. Afterwards we hauled the seal up. Some were very heavy — they can weigh up to two hundred pounds.

When the char were running upstream we'd make stone barriers. The fish swam through a narrow opening into a stone enclosure. We then filled the entrance with more stones so the fish were trapped. Then they were easy to spear. We caught and dried them on the side of the river.

Caribou

In this picture there are wolves, caribou, and people crossing the river. The wolves can't catch the caribou in the water. But the people are able to hunt caribou in their kayaks.

The caribou used to gather in a very large herd to migrate. You could hear them coming for two days, walking over the frozen tundra. We would sit where they would pass and wait for them. It would take three to five days and nights for the herd to pass our camp. The land would be all torn up. They were not afraid in such big numbers. We would walk among them and pick out the fat ones. We would kill them carefully without frightening the herd. If we did not hunt caribou, they would multiply and there would become too many of them. Then they would suffer and starve until the herds were the right size again.

Inuit would never set up camp in the path of the caribou. We wanted them to go their proper way. If someone put up a tent near a path, the caribou would change their route. When the mines started, the caribou were frightened and they changed their path. The Kabloonaq thought that the caribou were being hunted too much and that there were only a few left. But the caribou had just taken a different path.

The caribou did a lot for us. They gave us clothing and food. And we used them for our boats and sleds. The sinew made rope. The antler was used to make hooks. The bones were good for needles. Nothing was wasted. Blood was used for clothing dyes; tendons for thread. Their skins made our tents. The lighter skin was used in the tent to let in light. The bladder was used for bags to hold lard. Even the fat could be chewed to make candles or burned in a stone lamp. We did not even need to eat vegetables or grains. The raw meat and organs of the caribou provided everything that a body needed to live.

28

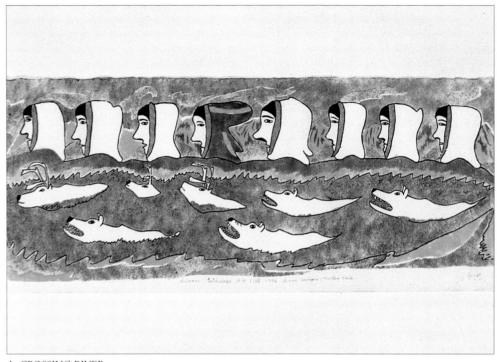

♦ CROSSING RIVER

When Inuit kill an animal in the traditional way, they give it a drink of water or, if there is no water, they melt snow with their mouths. The water is very helpful. Water eases the animal's suffering even after it is dead.

We also removed the sinews before we cracked the leg bones. This was also to ease the dead animal's pain. The spirit of the animal was grateful. We respected the animals and the animals allowed us to catch them. After we killed a caribou, the tradition was to point the skin towards your home or tent. It sent more caribou that way. It was the same when we fished at an ice hole. We took the fish heads and pointed them towards the hole to bring more fish to our line.

♦ INUKSHUKS

30

Inukshuks

Inukshuks are piles of stones in the shape of a person. They are all over the land. You can see them for a long distance. They have many purposes. Even if you have not been to a certain area, the *inukshuk* is a marker that will tell you what you need to know.

The Inuit could tell where the caribou were by the *inukshuks*. The rocks showed the people where the caribou would pass on their way south or north. They also directed the caribou to move in a certain way, like a herder. Inuit put moss on the top of the *inukshuks* to look like hair so the caribou would think they were people.

Inukshuks stood at places where the people camped. *Inukshuks* on a hill were used as lookout points for caribou. So we waited there to see them. *Inukshuks* by the river showed the path that caribou would take to cross the river. Now people build *inukshuks* as markers for their snowmobiles in case they get lost on the land. The *inukshuks* direct them home.

Rocks that were piled together near water were markers for fishing. We measured the distance they stood from the shoreline — that was the same distance we went into the water to jig for fish.

♦ MEETING A LONELY MAN

Old Things

I have found many old things on the land. I have found soapstone lamps and kayaks from the old people who used to live there. I found some things that belonged to the Tuniit, the people who lived on the land even before the Inuit. I did not take these things. It is the Inuit way to leave them alone.

Sometimes I come to a grave on the land. The graves are stones built up over the body because the ground is always frozen and hard to dig. I do not touch the stones out of respect, and I always leave a gift to its spirit. It depends on what the person wanted. Dying people used to say what they wanted from those who passed by. There is one grave where you make a gesture — pull the skin of your eyes because the person said he wanted people to open their eyes when they passed by. Sometimes I give small gifts when I pass a grave; even if it is just a bit of food, I drop it on the ground near the grave. That, too, is the Inuit way.

Sometimes people sit by the graves to get wisdom. This is also good for the spirit because it is lonely. It doesn't matter if you knew the person or not. You approach from the left and walk in a circle, then stand, and then finally sit. It clears the mind. It brings peace and wisdom.

People used to see ghosts often in the old days. This is because they worried about their dead ones more back then. The spirits felt pity for them and would appear as ghosts. There is nothing to fear from them. They are protecting spirits. People stopped grieving as deeply when Christianity took over. They stopped worrying so much about the dead because they believed that their spirits went to a better world.

Spirits in the World

A shaman (*angakok*) could be a man or a woman. Every shaman was different. Some were very troublesome; others were good and kind. It depended on the shaman's nature.

The good ones healed the sick. They could pull things out of the body without breaking the skin, things like caribou bones that caused the illness. They had many powers. They could fly and see beyond normal sight. They had great strength.

Shamans had many invisible creatures as friends and helpers. They were called *tungnaq* (spirit helpers). Shamans could put their spirits into these creatures. They could take the forms of birds or animals or even people. A shaman could tell his spirit helpers to hunt out his family and see if everyone was still well. The spirit helpers travelled across the land very fast and when they brought back what they saw, the shaman could see it, too.

Sometimes, a shaman would show you magic and make you forget. You would not remember the magic until he reminded you. Shamans had great power in many camps. They could make a tent shake.

When I was a boy I saw a shaman flying. We were in a tent a day north of Baker Lake. It was a quiet morning. I heard a great wind and went outside. My parents were still sleeping. I saw Teenaq, a shaman who lived far away. He was flying right over

my head the height of a low-flying airplane. He circled over the tent twice and
made sure that I saw him. I knew him well.
We had lived in the same camp. He shared
the same middle name as my mother. In
this way they were related. An hour later
he returned from another direction. He
circled one time and then he was gone.

I saw this man again in the fall. Late
one night he asked me if I remembered
seeing him fly. I said, yes. He asked me if
I was afraid. I said, no, I was not afraid. He

♦ SHAMAN'S FISH

said he had told my mother that he would be doing this and that he flew low so that
my mother would see him. He was going to his relatives whom he knew were in
some sort of trouble. The distance that he had travelled in that one hour was equal
to four days' travel by dog sled from early in the morning until late at night.

♦ BECOMING A SHAMAN

My Uncle Was a Shaman

My mother's brother was a shaman. He was named Oohuluaq. He was blind. I used to go fishing and hunting with him. I would point his weapon and tell him what I saw. He knew just when to strike or shoot.

He was very special to me, and I was special to him. I used to bring him to a fishing hole near the igloo so that he could fish. Sometimes my uncle would go home alone by feeling the frozen footprints in the snow with a stick. He could make an igloo by himself. He would tell me, "If you go hunting, even if you don't catch a caribou, keep hunting, never give up."

36

He had become blind as he got older. He could even hunt a caribou blind. I would go hunting with my uncle. I had a .22 rifle and hunted inland. I would stand beside my uncle, and he would tell me what to look for and what to do and when to shoot the caribou. Then he would teach me how to cut the meat and how to save it in a cache underground. I was his eyes and he was my mind. He showed me how to live.

When people were sick my uncle would fix them. He could pull the sickness out of the person's heart and bones. There was a time when I was very sick. I was bleeding from my nose a lot and it wouldn't stop. My parents were afraid that I would die. I was getting very weak from this bleeding.

My uncle told me that if I saw something strange, not to be afraid. I didn't understand what he meant. Then I went to another igloo that we used for a toilet room. It was sunset and the sun was very bright in my eyes as it came through the doorway. I looked into the sun and saw the shadow of a polar bear coming right at me. The bear did not seem to have a mouth. It came very near and pressed close to me. It began to lick my face. I was not afraid. I did not move or cry out. Then my face was clean. My nose stopped bleeding and the bear went away.

When I returned to the igloo my uncle examined me for blood and then began to laugh. He asked me, "Did you get scared?" I said, "No, I was not afraid." He asked me what I saw and I told him. He had red on his face but it was not blood. That is how I knew he had done magic on me. My uncle's magic made the polar bear. It was his spirit helper. It had cured me. After that I never had trouble with bleeding again.   37

♦ SHAMANS FIGHT

The Fight Between Shamans

Once we were camped with others. My father needed a tent very badly but there was no extra tent among his relatives. A shaman named Alikumiq wanted a dog. My father and this man traded. Later, the dog died and Alikumiq wanted the tent back. He threatened my father that he would kill him by magic.

My mother heard everything but she would not talk about it. She would not repeat anything bad about a person. My uncle was not there but he knew right away what happened. He told my father not to be afraid. He said that he would protect him.

Some time later, my father went hunting alone on the ice floe near the water. Alikumiq came by. He was fifty feet away but he began to push my father into the water by using a spirit helper. It was a wolf spirit. My father could not stop from being pushed. Suddenly, Alikumiq fell into the water. He was pushed by my uncle's magic. My uncle was back at the camp, sitting in the tent but he sent one of his spirit helpers to push Alikumiq into the water. It was a tree spirit that spun across the ground. Its name was Keepaluk. My uncle said to my mother in the tent, "There! I have helped my brother-in-law."

Alikumiq fell under the ice and stayed under the water for a long time. It seemed that he died. Then Alikumiq's body rose up out of the water and came onto the ice. He came to life. Alikumiq had used another spirit helper to do this.

After this Alikumiq was afraid of my uncle. He came to my father and promised never to try to hurt him again. My father did not trust him and we moved away. We never lived near him again.

Death Far Away

My uncle, Oohuluaq, asked my mother if he could teach me the ways of the shaman but she said no. She had become a Christian. The Church did not want our people practising the old ways. Also, I was the youngest and the last child staying with them. She said that a shaman's life is very hard on the body and on the mind. Shamans must be alone a lot and go for long times without sleep. They work with powerful spirits and must go through difficult changes. They do not live a long life.

She told my uncle not to teach me about shamanism but he did teach me much about animals. I am always thinking about animals. I know their ways and I am never afraid of any of them.

My uncle was taken away by the Kabloonaq who wanted to fix his eyes. We never saw him alive again. Everyone has to die.

After a long time they brought back his body and it was buried here. I was out on the land and I never saw him buried. The people are often taken south to Winnipeg or Churchill. They do not die with the people. They die alone in a strange place and then we get the body. I am not happy about this.

I could feel when my uncle died. It was then that I took his words and put them into my heart. He told me to always love people. Always be friendly to people. Share even if you are hungry. It does not matter whether they are Inuit or Kabloonaq. Though my uncle was blind, he always kept helping other people.

I had some of the power of my uncle. I used to know what was happening before it happened. But the only time I saw things up ahead was when someone was going to die or be hurt. When I saw something ahead to be happy about, then I could not wait for it to come. So I stopped trying to see any of these things.

Blizzard — The Unexpected

♦ ARRIVING AT IGLOO

When I was a young man I went out hunting and became lost in a blizzard. The day was fine but the storm came very quickly. In a storm you can watch the drifting snow to tell the directions because the wind usually comes from the north. But in a blizzard the wind keeps changing directions, so you must look at the hardened drifts to tell the way. In this storm it was too dark to see the drifts.

I had caribou clothes on so I stayed warm. I built a small igloo very quickly — it took less than half an hour. I would not build one near a hill because the snow could pile over it and, if the snow was very high, I could be deeply buried and suffocate. Also, I always make a small breathing hole.

The heat from your body melts any cracks and seals the walls of the igloo tightly. It is warm inside. It is like living in a big balloon underneath the snow with no light.

Sometimes it is necessary to stay inside many days. But in that blizzard, I cut through the igloo and the snow the next morning. The land had changed and the storm was still blowing, but I found my way home.

41

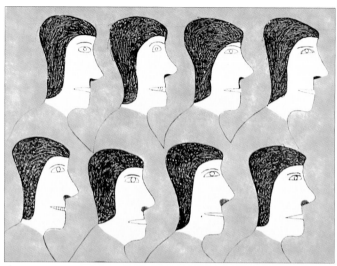

♦ SINGING NORTHERN LIGHTS

Northern Lights

The *arqsat* (northern lights) can get so bright that you can use them to travel by night. Some Inuit from other areas believed that the lights were the spirits of the dead chasing a ball across the sky. The spirits were playing soccer using the head of a muskox for a ball. If you whistled, you might bring them too close and the ball could knock off your head. We did not believe this.

However, the lights can be dangerous. They will follow you like a dog. You can make them come closer just by whistling. No one should try this because the lights are powerful. They sound like the wind or like a grizzly and they will frighten your dogs. I make a certain whispering sound like I do when I send away the dogs or else I rub my fingernails against each other. Then the lights back off. They are very beautiful but they are like dangerous water.

Danger Came Back to Me

Danger came back to me later, when I was a married man. I had been travelling by dog sled for two days and two nights without sleeping because it was spring and it did not get dark. I had seven dogs. All of them were well-fed and strong.

I was travelling at the floe edge. The ice was moving as it melted. I had to be careful because the ice can crack and crash upwards.

It was snowing and the snow covered the melting ice. I broke through the ice. I tied the rope to the sled and pulled it out with the dogs. It was very cold and I was very wet. I was so tired I could not keep running beside the sled. At times I had to lie on the sled. I had to get to the Kabloonaq settlement before I got too tired and froze. I told myself that I did not want to die yet. I gave myself the strength to keep struggling.

I reached the settlement and entered a house. The people took off my clothes. They were frozen solid. They gave me a little whisky to warm me up. It was the afternoon but it was late at night before I felt warm. The next day the Mounties gave me some of their clothes to wear so that I could return to my home on the land. When I arrived home the people came out of their igloos. They watched me coming but thought I was a Mountie — even my wife. They were all very surprised when they saw it was me.

First Seeing the Kabloonaq Homes

I was fourteen when I first visited the Kabloonaq settlement at Baker Lake. They had an Anglican and a Catholic church, as well as a trading post and a government station.

When I first entered a white man's house, I was eighteen. I did not like it. It was too hot and too bright. It was also very noisy — if something fell on the hard floor it made a big noise or if I bumped something it would clatter. Even my footsteps were loud. I was really surprised.

I was scared to be inside. Everything was washed and shining. I felt that I was unclean. I was wearing my caribou parka and I was worried that the heat would make the hair fall out. This always happened when the weather got warm in the summer and it was like summer inside the house.

The food seemed very strange. I remember getting an orange from the Hudson's Bay manager. It tasted awful and I spit it out. My only food was bannock, biscuits, and raw caribou meat. That was all I needed to be healthy.

In the weather station, I saw a TV. There was a cowboy show on and it scared me. I didn't understand the pictures in the box. I saw the cowboys shooting and I thought that they had killed each other. I thought the white people all fought like this.

♦ THINKING OF ANIMALS

I also saw a pet cat for the first time. It was frightening to see such a creature, more frightening than a wolf or a bear. The body was so small but the eyes were big and glowing. And the iris had such a strange shape. I thought it was a spirit creature.

The Kabloonaq wanted me to sleep in the house. I would not stay inside at night. I went out and built myself an igloo. But even in the igloo I could not sleep because I was afraid the cat would come out and get me.

When I was nineteen, I saw my first airplane. We were on the land and we did not know what it was. At first we thought it was some sort of bird. It was a bush plane. It came over our heads and we were very frightened.

45

♦ THE RESOUNDING BEAT OF THE DRUM

Qaggiq

Sometimes there was a calling together. Sometimes it was to celebrate the start of a journey when the people would separate into small groups. Other times it was to celebrate the end of a journey when the people came together again.

The people built a very big igloo made especially for drum dancing. It was called a *qaggiq* (a place of drumming). It could hold fifty people. They would make the roof out of snow, or for a very big roof they would tie their dog sleds together.

There would be a great meal, and then the people would begin to sing, "A ya! A ya!" Someone would pick up the *qilaut*, a hand-held drum made from the throat skin of a walrus or the intestines of a caribou. The person would beat it and start to dance. The dancing could go on all night. Sometimes it went on for twenty hours.

Someone would yell your name and you would take the drum. If two people had the same name they would both come up. Then there was a friendly struggle. Who would take the drum and sing? The winner was the one who had more of the name's power.

In this picture the people are in a circle listening to the beating of the drum. A story is being sung about dogs that are fighting wolves to protect the people.

Every person used to have special songs. One person would make a song about hunting. Another would make a song about an important experience, like meeting with a spirit.

My mother was teaching me a song for drumming, but the missionaries told us to stop. They thought it was a shaman's teaching. It was the song that she had been given by her grandfather. My mother knew many songs. She was a Keeper of Songs for the people. Some people still sing the songs she taught.

Group Decision Making

During the late summer when we would hunt for caribou, the people would come together to decide together who would hunt where. The old men and women and the best hunters made the decision. It took a day or two. The old people would stay behind because the hunt would be difficult for them.

We always respected the old people. They knew what was right. Sometimes if things became very bad and there was not enough food, an old person would insist on being left behind. This meant death. The old person did this for the good of everyone else. No one wanted this and people would agree only if things were very desperate and after much prodding.

The Starvations

In the winter of 1957 to 1958, the caribou took a different route to the calving grounds. We could not find them. All the animals were scarce. We were left waiting and many of the people died of hunger. There were five camps I know of with perhaps one thousand people altogether. They all starved to death.

My family did not suffer as much as others. None of us died. We kept moving and looking. We survived on fish. We had thirty dogs. All but four died but we only had to eat one of them. The rest we left behind. We did not feel it was right to eat them or to feed them to the other dogs.

♦ DREAM OF HUNGER

My father and his brothers had gone ahead to hunt. We had lost a lot of weight and were very hungry. I left the igloo and I knelt and prayed at a great rock. This was the first time I had ever prayed. Then five healthy caribou appeared on the ice and they did not run away. I thought I would not be able to catch them because there were no shadows. The land was flat without even a rock for cover. However, I was able to kill them with little effort. I was so grateful that I shook their hooves as a sign of gratitude because they gave themselves up to my hunger. I melted the snow with my mouth and gave them each a drink. I was careful in removing the sinews so as to ease their spirits' pain. This is the traditional way to show thanks. Because of what those caribou did, I always hunted in this way. I respected the animals.

For many years I was troubled by the memory of the Starvations. I had this recurring dream. Sometimes a dream will follow a person all day long until the person pays attention to it. This is the way it was for me with this dream. I felt it had to be made into a story or a picture.

This is the picture. It is January. These people are hungry. There are only two dogs left to pull the sled. The woman must pull and the man must push. There is no choice. The Inuit say *ajurnamat*, which means "it can't be helped." The child is too small to walk but too big to be carried in the back of an *amautiq* (a woman's parka). He is wrapped up on the sled.

49

♦ CREATION

Leaving the Land

I stayed on the land longer than the rest because I liked the land. I did not want to live like the Kabloonaq. I wanted to be free and live as my people always did before. It was lonely because there were only twenty of us together left on the land. All the rest had moved into the settlements.

A social worker landed by RCMP plane near our igloos and came out to tell us that we must go to the settlements like all the others and that the children must go to school. The Inuit were no longer supposed to live on the land. They said they would not let us have Family Allowance payments. This was the only money we had except for what we got for trapping — we needed that money to buy supplies. Still my wife and I decided not to go.

Later I left my son, Moses, who was eight or nine, with his uncle and went trapping. A plane landed near them and three people came out — a social worker, a Mountie, and the pilot. They took Moses away without telling anyone. We did not know what had happened to him. After a long time, we found Moses in the Baker Lake settlement. He was being kept in a residential school. He was being taught the Kabloonaq ways. He was not allowed to speak our language or learn our ways.

When I asked for him back I was told to stay away. Later I heard that Moses was being treated badly. My wife and I had to give up our life on the land and stay in the settlement — that was the only way they would let my son leave the residential school and live with me. I left the land and moved into the settlement in 1968 when I was thirty-four.

♦ ARGUMENT

52

Houses

The government told us not to live in igloos anymore — they gave us houses. I thought a house would be good because it was warm. I thought the walls would last forever and never get dirty.

But I also felt uncomfortable because the house didn't belong to me. I worried about damaging the floor with my caribou meat that I keep on the floor. We eat the traditional foods on the floor as we did in an igloo but we eat the Kabloonaq foods at the table or on the couch. We keep our caribou snow boots in the fridge to keep them from drying out. It is very warm for us in the house and bad for the meat — it thaws too fast and tastes bad. The igloo had a snow floor to keep things cool.

I worry about the furnace breaking down. We would quickly freeze. In an igloo, if there is no heat it stays the same temperature for a long time.

In a house everything is noisy. If I chop my food it is loud. I am surprised by sounds from different rooms and I disturb other people with my noise. And there are the sounds of the TV and radio.

People sometimes knock at the door to come in. That is not the Inuit way. There was no reason to knock on an igloo. There were not even any doors. I liked the way the igloo was always crowded and people were close.

I do not like having so many rooms. It doesn't feel good to have the children in another room at night — even when they are older. Now my children do not learn my thoughts or my stories. We do not talk as we would have on the land, in the igloo. It is because of the walls. Everyone goes to a different room. We do not talk all together anymore.

When I Draw

I first drew in 1971. The Kabloonaq paid me $5 for my first picture. I was very happy. I drew five more pictures and they took them all. At first I drew what I thought the white people wanted to buy. Later I began to draw what I wanted.

When I draw pictures, I think of the way it used to be when my people, the Inuit, still lived on the land. I think of legends. I think of my family at that time. I think of the shamans and I hear my uncle speaking to me in my mind. I remember my dreams. Sometimes when I draw it is like being in a dream.

In the old days the animals and the people were very much the same. They lived together on the land. They thought the same way and felt the same way. They understood each other. Shamans could even take on animal shapes or enter an animal and direct it to do their will.

When we fall asleep we dream and things that seem different join together — just like the animals and people once were joined together. This picture came to me in a dream. I realized that on the land, animals and people are one.

♦ THE WORLD OF PEOPLE AND THE WORLD OF ANIMALS MEET IN THE SHAMAN